B·O·O·K·S

From the Minds of Kids

By

Jennifer Weinstein

Columbus, OH

Photos: 35, © Karen Kasmauski/Corbis; **59,** © Bettmann/Corbis.

Illustrations: Denny Bond

SRAonline.com

 SRA

Send all inquiries to this address:
SRA/McGraw-Hill
4400 Easton Commons
Columbus, OH 43219

Printed in the United States of America.

ISBN: 978-0-07-611304-0
MHID: 0-07-611304-3

3 4 5 6 7 8 9 MAL 13 12 11 10 09 08

Contents

Chapter 1

Why Do People Invent?

Do you ever wonder where things come from? Have you ever thought to yourself, "Who decided to put wheels on a boot and zip around town?" or "Mmm, this frozen ice pop is so refreshing. I wonder who came up with this idea."

Inventors are people who create new things. They invent devices that make everyday life easier. They create new foods or new ways of preparing old foods. Inventors develop toys, clothes, tools, cars, and many other things we use every day.

Have you ever had a difficult math problem to solve or a pen that just wouldn't work? Did you ever want to do something fun, but had already played all of your games countless times? Then you have an idea about why people invent.

People invent for many different reasons. Some inventions are created to solve a problem. Others are created to do things faster, easier, or for less money. Some inventions are made to make life easier, safer, or more fun. Some inventors even take things that have already been invented and improve them.

So who are these inventors? Some inventors are famous, like Thomas Edison, Alexander Graham Bell, and Eli Whitney. Other inventors are just people who get an idea. Some inventors are even children!

Young children and teens have invented many of the things we use today. Just like adult inventors, these children saw a need and created something to meet that need. Some were trying to solve a problem, some were looking for a more exciting way to have fun, and some were just completing a school project.

Everywhere you go in the United States, you can find the U.S. flag. You know the U.S. flag has 50 stars that stand for the 50 states. But who designed that flag? Believe it or not, a teenager designed the current 50-star U.S. flag!

In 1948 Robert Heft was a 17-year-old high school student. Heft's social studies teacher wanted his students to create a project for class. At the time, there was talk of allowing Alaska and Hawaii to become part of the United States. This would bring the number of U.S. states from 48 to 50. Heft decided to use this as the starting point for his project.

In 1776 the original flag of the United States had 13 stripes and 13 stars. As new states became part of the United States, more stars and stripes were added to the flag. In 1818 Congress stated that the flag should always have 13 stripes to stand for the 13 original colonies. They also said the number of stars on the flag should equal the number of states.

*Heft knew the design of the U.S. flag had not changed since 1912. He wanted to change the design, but carefully. He did not want the change to be too obvious. So Heft took his parents' 48-star flag and cut it apart. Then he carefully arranged 50 stars on a new blue background. It took him over 12 hours to carefully arrange and sew the new flag.

Heft turned his project in to his teacher, who said it lacked imagination. Heft earned only a B-minus for his project. The teacher told Heft he could earn a better grade if he could get his flag adopted by Congress. So Heft took his idea to his congressman, who then took it to Congress. On July 4, 1960, Heft's flag was adopted as the new flag of the United States.

Since then, Heft's original 50-star flag has flown over the White House, over* every state capital, and in many different countries.

Heft took something that had already been designed and changed it to create something new. His idea came from the need to create a class project. Other inventors get their ideas because they need to solve a problem.

In 1994, when she was ten years old, Kathryn Gregory encountered such a problem. She was playing in the snow with her younger brother. Even though she had dressed for the cold weather, she found that snow was getting between her gloves and the sleeves of her coat. Her wrists were wet, cold, and sore.

When she went into the house, her mother suggested that Gregory sew something to help keep the snow out of her sleeves. With her mother's help, Gregory sewed a warm material called "fleece" into two tubes. She made each tube long enough to cover her hand and lower arm. Then she cut a hole in each tube for her thumbs.

Gregory made her invention to go under the sleeves of her coat, but over her gloves. She pulled the fleece tube over her gloves and poked her thumbs through the holes. The tubes covered her hands and lower arms, but kept her fingers free. Then it was time to test her invention.

Inventors usually have to test their inventions many times. They must make certain the invention works the way it should. In Gregory's first test, she found that the snow would get under the edge of the fleece tube and pile up on her palm.

What do inventors do when their inventions fail the first test? They don't give up! Inventors must often try many times before they get their inventions just right.

Gregory went back into the house and found a way to make her invention better. She made the fleece tubes smaller so she could wear them under her gloves instead of over them.

In her second test, Gregory found the smaller tubes worked well to keep her wrists dry and warm. She made fleece tubes for her friends, who loved them. Gregory knew she had a great idea.

After an inventor finds a winning idea, she or he has to do some more work. Gregory did some research and worked with a lawyer to make sure nobody else had invented the same thing. Then she gave her invention a name—*Wristies.*

Gregory started her own company—*Wristies, Inc.*—and is waiting for a patent for her invention. A *patent* gives an inventor the right to be the only person to make a certain item.

In 1997 Gregory became part of the Kids' Hall of Fame. She has also won several other awards. She often speaks at schools and invention workshops. Her success shows how even a child can turn an idea into a successful business.

Gregory used her invention to start her own company at the age of ten. Other young inventors find they enjoy entering their inventions in contests held in their schools and throughout the country. Some inventors, like Jeri Lee, enter these contests year after year.

Lee was in third grade when she discovered she enjoyed inventing. At that time she was facing a problem. Her dog kept hiding his dish, and she couldn't find it at feeding time. Lee put her problem-solving skills to work and came up with the *Feeder Keeper.*

She made a hole in the bottom of her dog's dish and put a long screw through it. Then she twisted the screw into the ground to keep the dish in place. She entered her invention in her school's invention contest and won first place.

Lee entered the school contest again each year she could. Her inventions continued to win prizes. In fourth grade she won third place with her *Handy Hair Bow Holder*. In fifth grade her invention won first prize. The invention, called *Freedom*, allowed Lee to swim while keeping the cast on her broken arm dry. In seventh grade she won first prize and was named Inventor of the Year for her invention to help blind people find their way around new buildings.

Eighth grade was the last year Lee could enter her school's invention contest, so she wanted to come up with a really great idea. She made a list of problems she needed to solve. One of these problems was her asthma. People with asthma have trouble breathing when there are certain things in the air like smoke or perfume. Lee decided to create a meter that would sound an alarm when these things were in the air.

She did a lot of research and came up with a plan for making the *Asthma Meter*. She won first prize in her school contest, was named Inventor of the Year once again, and won another invention contest for the state of Texas. Her Asthma Meter has not yet received a patent, but she hopes someday people will be able to use it.

— Chapter 2 —

Inventions That Help

Some inventors come up with ideas to solve a problem and help others with the same problem. Sometimes the things people invent help future inventors as well. Lee's invention for helping blind people would not have been possible without an earlier invention by a 15-year-old French boy named Louis Braille.

Braille was born near Paris, France, in 1809. When he was a small boy, he was playing with one of his father's sharp tools. The tool slipped and badly hurt one of Braille's eyes. By the time he was four, his other eye had become infected, and he lost his eyesight forever.

*As Braille grew older, he began attending school with his friends who could see. After two years it was clear Braille would not be able to learn much more. Most people at that time believed blind people could never learn to read or write because they couldn't see. Without reading and writing, these people could not be taught in school. Most blind people spent their lives begging on the streets.

When he was ten, Braille was sent to a school in Paris for blind boys. This school was one of the first of its kind in the world. The boys at the school were taught things that could help them later in life. They learned simple trades so they would be able to make a living when they left the school.

At the school, the boys were also taught a different type of reading. The man who started the school* had invented a system of making raised letters on paper. The children would feel the raised letters and figure out what was written.

12

Because making the raised letters was difficult and took a long time, the children were never taught to write. Braille thought there must be a better way for blind people to read and write.

In 1821, when Braille was 12 years old, a soldier came to visit the school. He showed the students a system of writing he had invented. This writing was made up of 12 raised dots. Each position of the dots related to a letter. The soldier could feel the dots in order to read in the dark. He called this system "night writing."

Braille realized this system of writing could allow blind people to read and write. Night writing had been too complicated for use in the army, but Braille thought he could make it simpler.

Braille created a system that used six dots rather than 12. Using a needle, he punched dots into a piece of paper. The dots formed a two-by-three arrangement. The positions of the dots in the arrangement made up a code. People could read by feeling the dots with their fingers. This system would also allow anybody to write using simple tools. Braille worked on his system for several years. He finally perfected it when he was 15 years old.

Braille taught this system of reading and writing to his classmates. The other boys were excited to use Braille's system, which became known as *Braille*. The school, however, did not allow the students to use Braille. This only made the boys more interested in learning it. When Braille was 17, he became an assistant teacher at the school and secretly taught Braille to his students.

In 1827, at the age of 18, Braille published the first book in Braille. This book taught people how to read using his system.

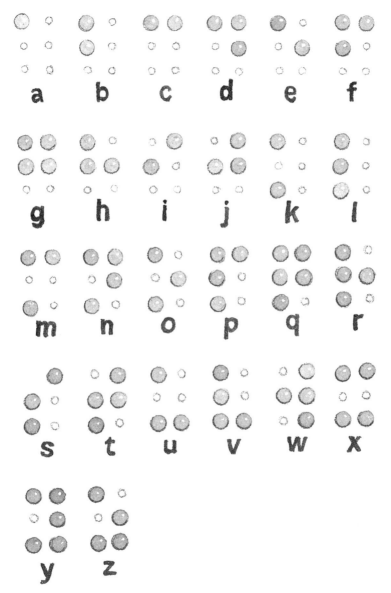

a b c d e f

g h i j k l

m n o p q r

s t u v w x

y z

15

Braille's invention made the world better by allowing blind people and people with low vision to read and write. Today, this invention by a 15-year-old boy is used in almost every country in the world.

Like Braille, many inventors get their ideas by trying to solve a problem of their own. Krysta Morlan knows what it is like to have a disability. When she was three, doctors found she had a condition called cerebral palsy. A person with cerebral palsy has very weak muscles.

When Morlan was in ninth grade she had a series of operations to improve her condition. After the operations, Morlan had to wear casts on her legs for almost a year. The casts went from her hips all the way to her ankles! In the summer heat, the casts were painful and uncomfortable. Morlan needed something to help her feel better.

There is a saying: "Necessity is the mother of invention." Morlan needed a way to feel better in her casts, so she decided to invent something. She thought it would help if she could get some cool air into the casts. So she came up with the idea of the *Cast Cooler*.

With her father's help, Morlan designed an invention that would blow cool air into a person's cast. The Cast Cooler uses a small pump and a battery-powered motor. The pump pushes cool air through a tube and into the cast.

Morlan entered her invention in a contest and won third place. In another contest, Morlan won the opportunity to work with a man who develops devices to help people with disabilities. He helped her create her next invention.

Morlan thought about what invention she should design. She remembered what she had been through in the past couple of years. After her operations, when the casts finally came off, Morlan had to do a lot of exercises. Exercising in a pool is a good way to make your muscles strong without hurting them.

She had thought these exercises were boring and decided to invent something to make them more fun. With the help of the professional designer, Morlan was able to do this.

First, Morlan learned how to make computer drawings of her idea. Next, she made a small copy of her idea to show what it would look like. Finally, she was able to build her invention. It was a *Waterbike!*

The bike was made out of lightweight materials that allowed it to float in the water. Morlan decided on the Waterbike because she loved being in the water and had not been able to ride a bike since her operations.

Morlan wanted people to be able to use her Waterbike for fun as well as for exercise. Much of the equipment people with disabilities have to use is very dull. Morlan thought young children would like the Waterbike because it is very colorful and fun-looking.

Both Morlan and Braille used their own challenges to invent things that could help others. While many disabilities cannot be prevented, safety devices can protect people from getting hurt in accidents.

Margaret Knight is most famous for her invention of the machine that makes square-bottomed paper bags. When she was 30 she became the first woman to receive a patent. Her inventing career, however, started at a much younger age.

As a young girl, Knight liked working with wood and tools more than playing with dolls. She often made sleds and kites for her brothers.

Knight's father died when she was young. Like many other children, Knight went to work at a local cotton factory when she was ten years old. When she was 12 years old, a piece of one of the machines in the factory broke off. It hit a young boy, and he later died from the injury. This accident upset Knight very much, so she decided to invent something that would prevent it from ever happening again.

Knight spent several days drawing and making small copies of her idea. Finally she came up with a device that would shut down a machine if it wasn't working right. Soon many cotton factories began using Knight's device to keep their workers safe.

When children put their minds to it, they can invent great things. Whether they make life easier, more comfortable, or safer, child inventors make the world a better place.

Chapter 3

Food and Fun Inventions

Imagine it is a beautiful summer day. The sun is shining; the sky is blue. And it's hot! You could really use a cold, refreshing treat. What do you ask for? If you lived in San Francisco in 1905, you might ask for an *Epsicle*.

The frozen ice pop we enjoy today was first called an Epsicle. In 1905, 11-year-old Frank Epperson invented this treat. Like many inventors, he discovered it by accident.

One evening Epperson was mixing himself a fruity drink on his back porch. At that time it was popular to mix sugary powder with water to create a sweet drink. By accident, Epperson left the drink on his back porch overnight.

That night the temperature dropped to a record low. When Epperson went out on the porch the next morning, he found that the drink he had mixed was frozen! The stick he had been using to stir the drink was stuck in it. He pulled out this ice on a stick and tasted it.

The treat tasted good, so Epperson showed it to his friends at school. The following summer, Epperson made Epsicles in his family's icebox. He sold them to local children, and they were a hit!

It wasn't until 18 years later, in 1923, that Epperson decided to apply for a patent on his invention. He began making seven different kinds of Epsicles. His children loved them and began asking for "Pop's sicles." Suddenly Epsicles had a new name—*Popsicles*.

Epperson received a patent for Popsicles the following year. Today there are more than 30 different varieties of Popsicles. What do you think is the most popular kind? It's orange!

Sometimes inventions are made by accident. Other times, a simple comment can inspire a person to invent.

Have you ever helped your mom or dad make bacon? It's a pretty messy procedure. You put the bacon in a pan and turn up the heat. Soon there's grease popping and splashing everywhere. The splashing grease can burn you. Besides that, the stove is soon covered with the slimy stuff.

Once the bacon is cooked, you don't want to eat all that grease. It's not healthy. So you lay the bacon on some paper towels to drain the grease. But what do you do if you're out of paper towels?

That is exactly what Abigail Fleck's father wanted to know. In 1993, when Fleck was eight years old, she was helping her father make breakfast. Her dad cooked the bacon and then realized they were out of paper towels. He had to use newspaper instead, which did not make Fleck's mother happy.

Fleck's father joked that he should let the bacon drip-dry. Suddenly, Fleck got an idea. What if she could find a healthier, cleaner way of making bacon?

Fleck worked with her father to design a dish that would cook bacon while the bacon hung over it. She made a square dish with three *T*-shaped bars above it. The bacon hung from the bars over the dish. Fleck called her invention *Makin' Bacon*.

Fleck's bacon-cooking dish could cook up to 18 slices of bacon at one time! Once she draped the bacon over the bars, she cooked it in a microwave oven. She placed a paper towel over the bacon so it didn't splatter, and the grease dripped into the dish. Fleck discovered that this way of making bacon was faster, cleaner, safer, and healthier.

Like Gregory, Fleck used her invention to start her own company. Since then she has received a patent for her invention. Newspapers and magazines have written stories about her. The stories tell about how Fleck decided on her invention and why it is a better way to cook bacon. She has even appeared on national television shows to talk about her invention.

Food inventions can make the world a better place. They offer treats and new, healthy ways of preparing old foods. And what goes better with food than fun?

*Children all around the world play games. Many children make up their own games. But it is very rare for these games to become popular with children and adults throughout the world.

Does the name George Parker mean anything to you? What about the name Parker Brothers? George Parker was the first of the Parker brothers to design and publish his own games.

Parker was born in 1867. He was the youngest of the three Parker brothers and wanted to be a writer when he grew up. As a child, Parker loved to play games. He even formed a game-playing club with his friends.

One day Parker and his brothers were playing a game together. They became bored with it, so Parker decided to change it. He created new rules and added cards to the game. He called the game *Banking*, and he, his brothers, and their friends continued to* play the game this new way.

Parker was 16 years old when he decided to publish the rules for Banking. He sent them to two book publishers. Both of them turned him down. But Parker didn't give up. He decided to publish the game himself. He spent 40 dollars to have 500 sets of Banking made. By the end of the year, Parker had sold all but 24 of the games. He had made 100 dollars profit!

With the help of his brothers and friends, Parker started his own game publishing company. He named it the *George S. Parker Company.* Parker invented all the games he sold and wrote all the rules for them.

By 1888 Parker's company was doing so well that his brother joined him. They changed the company's name to *Parker Brothers.* The brothers sold their games through a catalog. They had 29 games, and Parker had invented most of them.

Besides writing the rules for all of the games the brothers invented, Parker was in charge of finding ways to sell them. He did something nobody had ever done before. He placed ads in newspapers and magazines to sell his games. This approach worked well, and Parker Brothers became one of the leading publishers of games.

By the time Parker died at age 86, he had invented more than 100 games. Many of the brothers' games taught about things like money and American history. Parker Brothers games have been sold all over the world.

The company Parker started when he was just 16 became one of the largest and most successful companies in the world. Parker and his brothers made the world a better place by inventing different board games. Even today families play many of the games they invented.

Board games are a fun way to spend time indoors. What do you do, though, when your mom tells you, "Go play outside; it's a beautiful day"? You invent a new outdoor sport, of course!

Chapter 4

Sports Inventions

What kinds of things do you like to do on a hot summer day? Do you like to jump on a trampoline? Do you water-ski? How about in-line skating? In the winter, maybe you like to snowboard. Believe it or not, the equipment for each of these activities was invented by teenagers!

When George Nissen was a child, he enjoyed doing gymnastics and tumbling. He joined the school tumbling team in middle school and a local tumbling team in high school. Nissen also became involved in diving.

When he was 11, Nissen attended the circus with his family. He enjoyed watching the performers fly through the air. What he enjoyed most, though, was when they would fall into the safety net below.

From the net, the performers would bounce back up. They would continue performing, doing flips and turns in the air. Nissen realized that a similar device could be used to help gymnasts.

With a device like the safety net circus performers used, gymnasts could do complicated tricks. They would be able to perform moves like divers do, only without the water!

When Nissen finished high school at the age of 16, he set out to make his idea into an invention. He hunted in the local junkyard for materials he could use to make his "bouncing table."

In his parents' garage he built a frame and stretched a piece of strong material across it. Bouncing tables had been used before, but none had been made for people to buy and use in their own backyards.

For the next several years, Nissen worked to improve his bouncing table. Shortly after college, he and two friends took his bouncing table on the road. They used it to perform tricks for audiences in Texas and Mexico. While they were performing in Mexico, Nissen learned the Spanish word for "springboard"— *el trampolín.* Nissen now had a name for his invention—the *trampoline.*

Nissen took his trampoline all over the country, showing people how it worked and how much fun it was to use. After several years of hard work, he finally began selling many trampolines. He sold his invention to colleges, to families, and even to NASA!

George Nissen, inventor of the
trampoline, does a handstand

Nissen invented the first trampoline that could be used by families in their own yards. He got the idea by looking at something that was already being used and thinking about how he could change it. Some other outdoor activities people enjoy today were invented in a similar manner.

Have you ever skied down a mountain? The cold wind bites at your skin. The white, powdery snow sprays out behind you. The wind whistles in your ears. Many people enjoy skiing. They love speeding down a mountain and jumping through the air.

Snow skiing was the starting point for two other outdoor sports that are popular today. Waterskiing was invented by an 18-year-old. One of the first inventors of snowboarding was 13 years old. Both inventors used their interest in skiing as a starting point for a new invention.

Ralph Samuelson came up with the idea for waterskiing while he and his friends were snow skiing. He wanted to find a way to skim over the waves on skis.

Samuelson was already an expert aquaplaner. He would stand on a board called an *aquaplane* and hold on to a rope attached to a boat. While his brother Ben drove the boat, Samuelson would ride on top of the water on his aquaplane. Samuelson thought he could use the idea behind the aquaplane to design his water skis.

Samuelson spent five days in the summer of 1922 trying to invent a pair of skis that would work on the water. He and his friends had used pieces of wood to ski in the snow. He tried that, but it didn't work. He tried using snow skis. That didn't work either. Suddenly, Samuelson saw what the problem was. The front of the skis kept going into the water, causing him to fall on his face!

*Samuelson went out and bought two long, thin pieces of wood. He soaked one end of each piece in boiling water and bent the soft, wet wood. After the wood dried and hardened, he attached foot straps. Then he was ready to try waterskiing again.

Samuelson tied one end of a long rope to the back of his family's boat. With his brother driving the boat, Samuelson leaned back, ready to ski. He had decided to try keeping the tips of his skis pointed up. The boat took off, and soon Samuelson was skimming along behind it. On July 2, 1922, he became the first person to ever ski on water.

Samuelson took his water skis with him everywhere he went for the next several years. He skied in water shows and became the star performer. In 1925 Samuelson made the first water ski jump off a ramp. He also* skied behind a boat traveling at 80 miles per hour! He was the first speed skier.

It wasn't until the 1960s that people learned Samuelson was the father of waterskiing. Someone else had patented the idea before Samuelson was able to. In 1982 Samuelson was inducted into the Water Ski Hall of Fame in Florida.

Inventing new sports that combine winter and summer activities allows people to stay active year-round. When Tom Sims was ten years old, he was visiting his grandmother in California. Out in the street he saw something he had never seen before. Children were riding up and down the streets on skateboards.

Sims's father bought him his first skateboard, which Sims brought back to his home in New Jersey. Everything was fine until winter. Sims was not able to ride his skateboard in the snow. So when Sims was 13 years old, he decided to try something new.

In the winter of 1963, Sims was in his woodworking class. He asked his teacher if he could work on a project to make a ski board. His teacher agreed, and Sims's invention began to take shape. Sims removed the wheels from an old skateboard and added a sheet of thin metal to the front bottom of the board to make it slicker. He rode his board down little snow-covered hills in the winter. He rode his skateboard in the summer.

Sims continued to work on his design. By 1966 he had taken over his family's garage. He made his own skateboards and snowboards. After moving to California, Sims started a company that made skateboards. Today he owns one of the leading snowboard manufacturing companies in the world.

Snowboarding has become very popular. It has even become part of the Winter Olympics!

Like waterskiing, in-line skating also grew from a winter sport—ice-skating. In-line skates have been around since the 1700s. But the skates as we know them today were invented by a pair of brothers in 1978.

Scott and Brennan Olson loved to play ice hockey. In fact, everywhere Scott went he dreamed of skating. One day, shortly after finishing high school, Scott and his younger brother Brennan were in a store. They saw an old pair of roller skates hanging on a wall. But these skates were different. Instead of having four wheels in a box shape, the wheels were in a line straight down the middle of the skate.

Scott was excited! He realized that his dream of skating outdoors all year round could come true. He saw that by improving on the idea of putting the wheels straight down the middle of the boot, he would have more control of the skates. The brothers went home and got to work.

They took the boots from hockey skates and added a line of wheels and a heel brake. In the winter they put the ice-skating blades back on the boots.

The brothers were able to sell their new skates to neighbors. Soon other hockey players began buying them so they could continue training in the summer.

In 1980 the brothers started a company called *Rollerblades, Inc.* that made in-line skates. They sold their company in 1984. In-line skating became very popular throughout the country in the 1990s.

Nissen, Samuelson, Sims, and the Olson brothers brought new sports to the world. Their inventions gave people a way to have fun outdoors all year long.

Chapter 5

Very Young Inventors

Gregory was only ten when she invented Wristies, and Fleck was only eight when she invented Makin' Bacon. But can even younger children invent useful things? You bet they can!

Chelsea Lanmon was just five years old when she created her first invention. She was helping her mother change her baby brother's diaper when the idea occurred to her.

Lanmon saw how many things were needed for the simple task of changing a baby's diaper. She decided she could make the job easier by combining everything in one small pack. Lanmon decided to invent the *Pocket Diaper*.

Her idea was that each diaper would have its own pocket. A baby wipe and a powder puff could be stored in the pocket until the diaper was ready to be used. Then the pocket could be removed from the diaper and thrown away.

After trying and changing some of her ideas, Lanmon's final product was ready to go. She decided to enter her invention in a contest. But Lanmon didn't enter a school contest; she entered a national contest. And she won first place!

Lanmon was only in kindergarten, and she was being written about in newspapers and magazines. She even appeared on national talk shows. Lanmon received a patent for her design when she was eight years old.

She continued inventing throughout grade school. Every year she entered either a local or national invention contest. Some of her inventions include a device for ironing sleeves, a heated ice cream scoop, and a grease-fire detector for pans.

Jeanie Low was also in kindergarten when she made her first invention. She heard about an invention contest her school was having and decided to enter. But what would her invention be?

Low had been using a small step stool to reach the bathroom sink. The stool was not very stable. It could break, and it took up a lot of room in the bathroom. Low decided she would solve her step-stool problem and enter her invention in the school's contest.

Low's idea was to make a stool for small children that would be strong but wouldn't take up a lot of room. She went to a local store, and the people there helped her find the materials she needed. But they didn't really think a person so young would be able to build what Low had explained to them.

Low proved them wrong! She went home and built the *Kiddie Stool.* She used a hinge to attach one piece of wood to the cabinet under the bathroom sink. Using another hinge, she attached a second board to the first. When she opened the hinges, the boards formed a step stool. When she folded the boards back up, a magnet held the pieces against the cabinet.

Low's Kiddie Stool won first place in her school's contest. When she was seven, she entered her invention in a citywide contest. She won first prize again. In 1992 Low received a patent for her invention.

*If you go to a toy store and look at the baseball toys, you might see something unusual. It is a toy bat with a top that can be removed so you can store baseballs inside the bat. This toy was invented by a six-year-old boy trying to solve one of life's many problems. How do you keep from forgetting baseballs when you go out to play?

Jacob Dunnack went to visit his grandmother one day. Planning to play baseball, Dunnack brought his bat with him. Unfortunately, he forgot to bring baseballs. His grandmother thoughtfully tried to solve the problem by making paper balls. But it just wasn't the same. Dunnack needed more than a baseball; he needed a solution to the problem of forgotten baseballs.

Instead of wishing somebody would solve this problem for him, Dunnack set out to solve it himself. He thought about the problem and about* possible ways to solve it. Finally he came up with a solution—and an invention for a school contest.

On the way home from his grandmother's house, Dunnack told his mother about his idea. When they got home, Dunnack searched his family's garage for an old toy bat. He cut off the top of the bat and dropped a few baseballs into the bat. Then he sealed the bat with some foam and tape.

The first bat Dunnack made may have been rough, but his idea was a winner. Dunnack entered his invention in his school's invention contest. His teacher liked his invention so much she suggested he and his parents try to get a patent for it.

Dunnack is waiting for the patent. In the meantime, he and his parents have decided to sell his bat in toy stores. Dunnack's mother contacted a large national toy store. The store liked the invention and decided to sell it. And Dunnack got to make some big decisions.

He decided the bat should be blue—his favorite color. He also decided there should be three yellow balls inside the bat—one for each child in his family. Finally he decided on a name for his invention. He called it the *JD Batball*.

Dunnack, like other inventors before him, looked at a problem he had and found a way to solve it. Now children all over the country can be sure they don't forget their baseballs when they go out to play.

When she was six years old, Kelly Reinhart was playing with her six brothers and sisters. It was a rainy day, so the children were playing in the house. Trying to get some peace and quiet, Reinhart's parents asked the children to sit at the table and draw. They asked each of the children to draw a new invention.

Reinhart's parents told their children they would pick the best invention and try to make it. Reinhart remembered a movie her father had been watching in which cowboys were wearing holsters around their hips. She thought about how kids might use something similar.

Reinhart drew her invention—a pouch that could be worn around the thigh. Reinhart thought this would be a good invention for kids to use to carry their video games and other things.

Reinhart's parents also thought her idea was good, and she won the family's contest. Her parents asked a friend to sew a sample of the pouch. Reinhart took her pouch, which she called the *TPack*, to school. The kids loved it!

Reinhart and her parents got a patent for her design and had 100 TPacks made. Reinhart sold all of the pouches and used the money to have more made. Soon she was receiving orders for thousands of TPacks. Her father quit his job and began working full-time for her new company, *TPack International.*

Reinhart has talked to some pretty important people about her invention. She met with her congressman, the Secretary of the Army, and even the President of the United States! Since creating her invention, she has written a book for children about inventing. She has also taught other children how to take their ideas and make them into inventions. In fourth grade Reinhart was even allowed to take a class at a local college!

Sometimes people don't take the ideas of young children seriously. However, Reinhart, Dunnack, Low, and Lanmon proved that even the youngest children can have some pretty amazing and useful ideas.

Chapter 6

Invent It!

As you know, inventors get their ideas from a variety of places. Some ideas come from the need to solve a problem. Some ideas come from a stray comment. Some ideas come from the desire to help people. Some ideas even come from just having fun.

Richie Stachowski was on vacation with his parents when the idea for his invention came to him. Stachowski was 11 years old at the time. He and his father were out snorkeling, and Stachowski was excited by the fish he was seeing. He wanted to shout out to his father. But, of course, you can't talk under water. Or can you?

Stachowski thought there could be a way to talk to people under water. He asked his father, who was a diver, if anything had already been invented that allowed a person to talk to others under water. His father didn't know of anything like that. So, back in his family's hotel room, Stachowski began making drawings of his idea.

Once his family returned home from their vacation, Stachowski got to work. He used money from his savings account to buy materials. He took a snorkel mouthpiece and attached it to a sports cone. Then he began testing his invention in a swimming pool.

During the testing of his invention, Stachowski found he needed a way to keep water from flooding the cone and mouthpiece. He was able to fix that problem with a blow valve. The valve allows air to go out of the device without letting water in.

Stachowski spent another month perfecting his invention. Finally it was ready. He was able to use it to talk to another person up to 15 feet away—under water!

Stachowski called his invention *Water Talkies* and started his own toy-making company. He and his mother talked to people who bought toys for a large toy store. At the end of his speech explaining his invention, Stachowski showed them how it worked. He used one of his Water Talkies and a full fish tank to ask them to place an order. They did—for 50,000 Water Talkies!

Most inventors do not stop with just one invention. Stachowski continued to invent new products for his company. He likes to tell young inventors, "If you think you have a good idea, just go for it!"

Sometimes an idea seems so simple you wonder, "Why didn't I think of that?" Take earmuffs, for example. Earmuffs are a nice, simple invention, but they were not around before 1873.

*Chester Greenwood is the boy behind earmuffs. Greenwood came from a poor family. Born in 1858, he helped his family by delivering eggs. He would walk eight miles a day delivering eggs and selling candy he had made. Amazingly, Greenwood's idea for the earmuff did not come while he was traveling his long egg-delivery route.

One winter day, 15-year-old Greenwood went out to try a new pair of ice skates. By the time he reached the pond his ears were freezing. His scarf made his ears itch, so he rushed back home to find something else that would keep his ears warm.

Once home, he had an idea about how he could keep his ears warm. He asked his grandmother to help him sew some ear coverings out of fur. He used a soft wire to hold the coverings in place. When other children saw Greenwood's ear coverings, they began* asking their mothers and grandmothers to make some for them.

Even though the ear coverings were popular, Greenwood wasn't happy with them. So he worked to improve them. First he decided to use a kind of steel instead of wire to hold them on a person's head. Then he added a tiny hinge to the earflap so it would fit snugly against the ear. Finally he was happy with his invention. He called it the *Greenwood Champion Ear Protector*.

Greenwood's invention grew into a successful company. He opened a factory and ran the business himself. In addition to running his earmuff factory, he continued to invent. He received over 100 patents in his lifetime for his inventions!

Earmuffs seem like a simple idea. Inventing a calculator, on the other hand, would be a little more complicated.

In 1642, 19-year-old Blaise Pascal invented what we know as the first mechanical calculator. Pascal was born in France and moved to Paris with his family when he was eight years old. His father saw that Pascal was very smart, and he wanted Pascal to have the best schooling.

Pascal became very interested in math and science at an early age. Many of the ideas we learn about in math and science classes today came from young Pascal. He performed experiments to learn about the world. He also read books and discussed math with others. By the age of 14, he was meeting weekly with a group of men who studied math.

Pascal's father was a tax collector. He spent his days counting and adding. At that time, people were the only computers. Pascal's father would do all of the math by hand. Pascal wanted to invent a machine that would make his father's job easier.

Pascal went to work. He invented an adding machine called the *Pascaline.* The Pascaline was a box with five dials on it. The dials were connected in such a way that turning one dial ten times would cause the dial to its left to turn once. Think about how we add. If you add the ones place and the sum is ten or more, you must carry to the tens place. That's what the Pascaline did.

Pascal made the Pascaline in different sizes. Some had six dials, and some had eight. An eight-dial Pascaline was able to add up to the ten-millions place!